The World of
Whales & Dolphins

WWF
World Wildlife Fund

DAY DREAM
PUBLISHING INC.

WWF

World Wildlife Fund (WWF) is dedicated to protecting
endangered wildlife and wildlands around the world. Since its founding
in 1961, WWF has helped protect hundreds of plant and animal
species and preserve millions of acres of habitat on five continents.

Many whale species have been reduced by commercial whaling to small remnants of
their original populations. WWF helped persuade the International Whaling Commission (IWC)
to create an Antarctic Whale Sanctuary to protect the feeding grounds
of 90 percent of the world's remaining whales.

Hopefully, the Antarctic Whale Sanctuary will speed the recovery of some depleted whale populations.
Together with the Indian Ocean Sanctuary, the new sanctuary now makes more than one-third
of the world's oceans a permanent safe haven for these magnificent animals. WWF continues
to support the IWC's worldwide moratorium against commercial whaling.

For more information, please write to:

World Wildlife Fund
1250 24th Street, N.W., Dept. ZBL6
Washington, D.C. 20037

*S*trong against the tide, the enormous

whale emerges as he goes."

—Christopher Smart

Orca

T he defect that hinders communications between dolphins and us, why may it not be on our part as well as theirs? . . . We understand them no more than they do us; by the same reason, they may think us to be beasts as we think them."

—Michel de Montaigne

Atlantic spotted dolphin

"In a cool curving world he lies

And ripples with dark ecstasies."

—Rupert Brooke

Humpback whale

N o animal of the sea or land figures more frequently in the fanciful creations of the Greeks and Romans than the dolphin. It is represented in their myths as an attribute, symbol, companion, and servitor of the mighty gods, who were themselves not ashamed to borrow its form … To dream of this wonderful animal signified good …"

—Paul Biedermann

Atlantic spotted dolphins

*A*ll the whales suddenly reversed

themselves, and, elevating their broad

flukes in the air, commenced to beat them

slowly and rhythmically upon the water, like so many

machines."

—Frank T. Bullen

Humpback whale

"The whole school surrounded the ship and
. . . as if instigated by one common
impulse, they all elevated their massive heads above
the surface of the sea, bobbing up and down amid the
glittering wavelets like moveable boulders of black
rock."

—Frank T. Bullen

Pod of orcas

A whale learns with amazing rapidity,

developing such cunning in an hour or

two that all a man's smartness may be

unable to cope with his newly acquired experience."

—Frank T. Bullen

Humpback whale

or the space of a few minutes, they are capable of darting through the water with the velocity of the fastest ship under sail, and of ascending with such rapidity as to leap entirely out of the water."

—W. Scoresby Jr.

Bottlenose dolphins

*S*cattered on the surface of the sea, basking or

sleeping, spouting leisurely, and exhibiting

every indication of being 'at home' . . ."

— *Frederick Debell Bennett*

Humpback whale

C lose nestled by her side was a youngling of not more than five days old, which sent up its baby-spout every now and then about two feet into the air. One long, wing-like fin embraced its small body …"

—Frank T. Bullen

Humpback whale & calf

"O, *ye whales, and all*

that move in the waters …"

— Book of Common Prayer

Humpback whale

"*H*is bliss is older than the sun.

Silent and straight the waters run.

The lights, the cries, the willows dim,

And the dark tide are one with him."

—Rupert Brooke

Beluga whale

S portively brandish their broad and fan-shaped flukes in the air or protrude their heads perpendicularly above the waves, like columns of black rock."

—Frederick Debell Bennett

Humpback whale

We almost immediately beheld the whale—

a pale, shadowy column of white,

shimmering against the dark mass of a cliff …"

—Frank T. Bullen

Orca

"And the secret deeps are whisperless;

And rhythm is all deliciousness;

And joy is in the throbbing tide,

Whose intricate fingers beat and glide…"

—Rupert Brooke

Orca

The word 'dolphin' comes from the Greek
delphis or delphoi, meaning womb,
because the dolphin's young are born alive.

Bottlenose dolphin

"...***T***rue leviathan hugest of living creatures

on the deep stretch'd like a promontory

sleeps or swims ...."

—John Milton

Humpback whale

*L*ike an arrow they fly through the sea, and
fiery and keen is the light they flash from
their eyes ..."

—Oppian

Atlantic spotted dolphins

othing in the sea is faster than they are …

Humpback whale

"Genius in the sperm whale? Has the sperm whale ever written a book, spoken a speech? No, his great genius is declared in doing nothing in particular to prove it."

—Herman Melville

Orca

"The dolphin does not fear the elements,

nor distance, nor the sea's tyrants."

—Leclerc de Buffon

Atlantic spotted dolphins

"They are, in a way, land animals as well as water animals; they inhale the air, like land animals, but they have no feet and they get their food from the water as water animals do."

—*Aristotle*

Humpback whale

nuit myth claims the land is alive—

a whale harpooned when Raven Man

married … You can still see the wound—a

hollow in the tundra where the grass grows long.

Orca

*W*hat has ever caught the imagination more
than the dolphin? — light in his movements,
rapid in his swimming, astonishing in his jumps …

Spinner dolphins

"Being almost a perfect calm, every movement of the great mammals could be plainly seen. For over an hour they thus paraded around us, and then, as if starteld by some hidden danger, suddenly headed off to the westward, and in a few minutes were out of our sight."

— Frank T. Bullen

Humpback whale

"Whatever befalls the earth, befalls the sons of the earth. Man did not weave the web of life: he is merely a strand in it. Whatever he does to the web, he does to himself."

—Chief Seattle 1835

Humpback whale

PHOTO CREDITS